5

# ANCIENT EGYPT

# BUILDERS & CRAFTSMEN

Jane Shuter

**Heinemann Library**
**Des Plaines, Illinois**

© 1999 Reed Educational & Professional Publishing
Published by Heinemann Library,
an imprint of Reed Educational & Professional Publishing,
1350 East Touhy Avenue, Suite 240 West
Des Plaines, IL 60018

Designed by Clare Sleven
Illustrations by Jonathan Adams, Jeff Edwards
Printed in Hong Kong

03 02 01 00 99
10 9 8 7 6 5 4 3 2 1

Library of Congress Cataloging-in-Publication Data

Shuter, Jane.
    Builders and craftsmen / Jane Shuter.
        p.    cm. -- (Ancient Egypt)
    Includes bibliographical references and index.
    Summary:  Discusses the lives led by the people who built the
pyramids, tombs, and temples of ancient Egypt.
    ISBN 1-57572-728-5 (lib. bdg.)
    1.  Egypt--Civilization--To 332 B.C.--Juvenile literature.
2.  Building--Egypt--Juvenile literature.  3. Artisans--Egypt-
-Juvenile literature.  [1. Egypt--Civilization--To 332 B.C.
2. Building--Egypt.  3. Artisans--Egypt.]  I. Title. II. Series:
Shuter, Jane.  Ancient Egypt.
DT61.S6434    1998
932'.01--dc21                                                    98-9437
                                                                     CIP
                                                                      AC

## Acknowledgments

The Publishers would like to thank the following for permission to reproduce photographs: Ancient Art & Architecture: p. 12; British Museum: p. 19; E. T. Archive p. 17; Michael Holford: p. 7; Manchester Museum: p. 29; Christine Osborne Pictures: p. 28; Photo Archive: J. Leipe p. 27; Wellcome Trust, London: p. 15; Werner Forman Archive: pp. 13, 23

Cover photograph reproduced with permission of Michael Holford.

Any words appearing in the text in bold, **like this**, are explained in the Glossary.

# CONTENTS

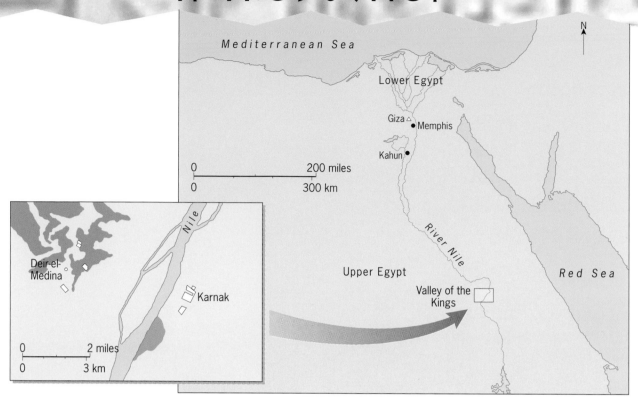

This chart shows different times in the long history of Ancient Egypt. The red blocks show when pharaohs were weak and no one ran the whole country.

When people think about Ancient Egypt, many of them think about the pyramids, **tombs**, and **temples** that lie along the Nile River. These were built thousands of years ago by people who had only very simple tools. But they had many skills and a lot of time. There were also many workers to help them.

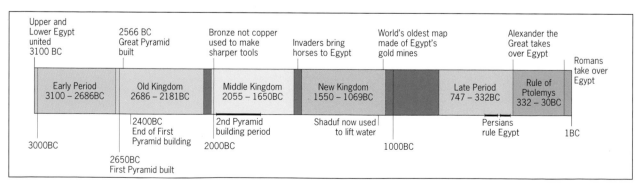

| Upper and Lower Egypt united 3100 BC | 2566 BC Great Pyramid built | Bronze not copper used to make sharper tools | Invaders bring horses to Egypt | World's oldest map made of Egypt's gold mines | Alexander the Great takes over Egypt | Romans take over Egypt |
|---|---|---|---|---|---|---|
| Early Period 3100 – 2686BC | Old Kingdom 2686 – 2181BC | Middle Kingdom 2055 – 1650BC | New Kingdom 1550 – 1069BC | | Late Period 747 – 332BC | Rule of Ptolemys 332 – 30BC |
| 3000BC | 2400BC End of First Pyramid building | 2nd Pyramid building period | Shaduf now used to lift water | | Persians rule Egypt | 1BC |
| | 2650BC First Pyramid built | 2000BC | | 1000BC | | |

## HOMES

Pyramids, tombs, and temples were built from stone and made to last. Ordinary homes were not. They were made from mud bricks and have long since crumbled away and been rebuilt. The only ordinary houses from Ancient Egypt to survive are in the desert. These villages were built for the people who worked on the pyramids and the tombs in the Valley of the Kings.

Huge stone temples and palaces were designed and decorated by experts. Most of the heavy stone hauling work was done by ordinary workers. Many of them did it as their corvée—the yearly work they had to do for the pharaoh.

Pyramids were **tombs** for **pharaohs**. They were built from 2700 B.C. to 1750 B.C. The first pyramids were built from stone. Later, they used mud bricks with a stone outer layer.

## HOW DID THEY BUILD PYRAMIDS?

**Priests** studied the stars to chose a pyramid **site**. They made sure the ground was level.

Workers dragged stones to the site from nearby quarries using sledges and ropes. They chipped the stones into shape with **copper** tools. The stone was brought from far away by sailing boats to the site during the **inundation**. Then the builders made the pyramid layer by layer. They added false doors, corridors, and hidden rooms to keep the pyramid safe from robbers. Earth paths wound up the sides of the pyramid as it was built higher so the builders always had a level platform. The outside layer was made of limestone rock. Builders checked that the sides were flat by dragging a rope covered in red soil across it. The rope caught on any bumps and made a red mark. The sides were smoothed and polished when the paths were cleared away.

## PYRAMID FACTS

- The biggest pyramid is the one built for Cheops in 2500 B.C. It is 479 feet (146 meters) high.
- It was made with about 2,300,000 stone blocks. Each block weighed about 2.8 tons, although some weighed as much as 16 tons.
- The base covered about 12.97 acres (the same size as about 200 tennis courts). Despite its size, it is an almost perfect square.

Only a small part of a pyramid was used for the corridors and rooms. The tomb was usually under ground!

# KAHUN

Workers building the pyramid of Sesostris II at Lahun (in about 1895 B.C.) lived at Kahun. The town was built especially for them.

## WHO DID THE WORK?

Most of the workers were men on **corvée**. Groups of five to ten workers hauled the stones. Others made mud bricks for the inside walls. The workers were paid in **grain** and beer. They worked in two-month **shifts** during the **inundation**. During the rest of the year, they farmed the nearby fields. There were also **architects,** craftsmen, and **officials** to run the building works.

## WHAT DID KAHUN LOOK LIKE?

The workers lived in rows of houses made from mud bricks and **whitewashed** on the outside. They had mud floors and wooden doors. Each house had four or five rooms and a set of steps to the roof. There were larger houses for the more important officials and **priests**. There was even a huge house with high walls and big rooms that the **pharaoh** may have used on his visits to check the building work.

The workers area of Kahun. There would have been fields on the other side of the town running down to the river.

**Pharaohs** were not always buried in pyramids. Some were buried in **tombs** cut deep into the rock in a place now called the Valley of the Kings.

## HOW DID THEY BUILD TOMBS?

**Priests** studied the stars to choose a tomb site. They had to be careful not to run into earlier tombs. They probably had maps for this, but none have survived.

Builders dug away the sand and loose rock. They cut into the rock and dug it out with wooden mallets and **copper** or **bronze** chisels. Most of the rock was limestone, which was easy to cut. But there were lumps of hard flint and the tools were not strong enough to chip them away. They had to leave them. As the workers went on, they kept measuring carefully to make sure the walls, roof, and floor were straight. Other people dragged the dug stone away in baskets. The tomb was lit with torches. Other workers who smoothed the walls, floor, and roof followed the stone cutters. They prepared for the painters who followed them.

Cutting tombs out of rock with simple tools and no lifting equipment was hard work. It was also hot and dusty work; the Valley of the Kings was on the edge of the desert.

The village of Deir el-Medina was built for workmen from the Valley of the Kings and their families to live in. Unlike Kahun, Deir did not have fields to farm. The workers worked on the **tombs** all year round. All of their food and water was hauled up to the village.

## WHAT DID DEIR LOOK LIKE?

The families lived in mud brick **terraced** houses. There were about 70 houses on either side of a main street. Each had four rooms and stairs to the roof. The doors were wooden and the floors were stone. There were no windows. Light came through slots in the flat roofs. The walls were **whitewashed** inside and outside. The tomb workers' own burial place was outside the village. They worked on this together in their spare time.

Deir el-Medina today. You can see the stone foundations (bases) of the workers' houses.

A painting from a worker's tomb. It shows people busy making coffins, mummy masks, and furniture for the tombs.

# WORKERS AND THEIR FAMILIES

The workers stayed near the tombs and worked for ten days at a time. They decorated the tombs and made things for them such as furniture and **tomb models**.

The workers' families stayed in Deir. The women ran the home and brought up the children. They did not work on the tombs.

WORKERS WERE PAID IN FOOD — MOSTLY GRAIN TO MAKE BREAD AND BEER. IF THEIR PAY WAS LATE, PEOPLE WENT HUNGRY. AT LEAST ONCE, THEY STOPPED WORKING AND WROTE TO THE **PHARAOH** THREATENING TO STRIKE BY COMPLAINING:

We are hungry and thirsty. We have no clothes, no fat, no fish, and no vegetables. We write this to the king, our good lord, so he will give us these things so we can live.

**Tombs** were not the only buildings that were made to last. **Temples** and official buildings were also built mostly from stone. They were often built together and walled off from the ordinary people. The **pharaoh** was the most important person in the running of the country and religion, so it made sense to have temples and official buildings close together. People's homes (even the pharaoh's) were usually made from mud bricks not stone.

A GREEK WRITER VISITED EGYPT IN 450 B.C. HE SAW THE TEMPLES AND PALACES OF SHEDYET, HOME OF THE CROCODILE-HEADED GOD, SOBEK:

The City of the Crocodiles is more amazing than the pyramids. It has twelve covered courtyards, six in a row facing north, six south, surrounded by a huge wall. There are about 3,000 rooms, half of which are underground. I saw the upper rooms, and it is hard to believe that men built them. They were built of stone and covered with beautiful carved figures.

Medinet Habu: the temple and palace buildings seen from the air.

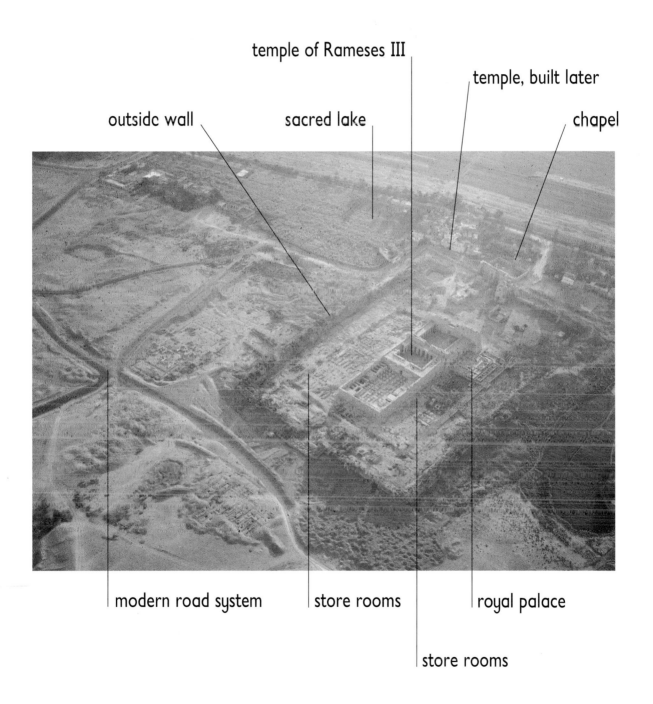

temple of Rameses III

temple, built later

outside wall

sacred lake

chapel

modern road system

store rooms

royal palace

store rooms

We are going to take a closer look at the **temple** of Rameses III at Medinet Habu.

## THE BUILDINGS

Like all Ancient Egyptian temples, the temple is surrounded by high walls. Two open **courtyards** are inside. A **ramp** goes from the second courtyard to the **chapels**, which were used for praying to various gods including the **pharaoh**, Rameses III, and the sun god, Amun. The main path leads straight to the **shrine** of Amun. Only the most important **priests** could go into shrines, so the shrine is small and dark. The temple, as well as chapels and the shrine, has a house for the pharaoh's use and rooms for storing the "royal treasure."

## THE DECORATIONS

The temple is covered with carvings and many of them show important events in the life of Rameses III. The carvings are still there today, but the gold and silver decorations and the paint have mostly worn away.

A small part of the temple of
Rameses III today. The
carvings would have been
beautifully decorated.

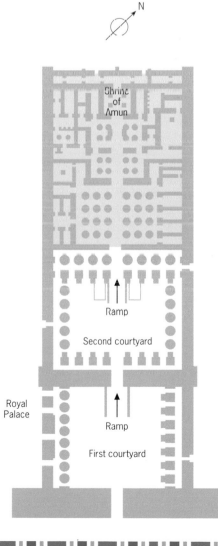

N

Shrine
of
Amun

Ramp

Second courtyard

Royal
Palace

Ramp

First courtyard

A plan of the whole temple. Everything
would have been decorated.

Egyptian towns were built from mud bricks. They were surrounded by farmland that was low enough to be flooded by the Nile River during the **inundation**. The towns were built on raised land so that they were not flooded during the inundation—unless the Nile flooded far more than usual.

## WORKERS' HOMES

Ordinary people lived in white painted **terraced** houses with four or five rooms. Holes in the walls let in light. These houses had flat roofs. People spent a lot of time on the roof, even cooking and eating there. For shade, they had **awnings** or plants grown over a frame.

A GREEK WRITER VISITED EGYPT IN 450 B.C. HE SAW THE INUNDATION:

When the Nile overflows, the whole country is turned into a sea. Only the towns stay above water, like islands. People sail all over the country, not just up and down the river. You could even sail right up to the pyramids.

## OFFICIALS' HOMES

More important people had houses built around a **courtyard.** The courtyards were full of plants and often had a pond. Big houses were painted white and had decorations painted over the top. The doors were wooden. The windows were small and high and had wooden shutters.

In this picture, a **scribe** and his wife pray to the god Osiris. Their house is behind them. The artist drew the courtyard in front of them. In real life, the courtyard would have been in the middle of the house.

Ancient Egyptian towns were crowded and busy. They were near the river with farmland all around. People who lived in towns did all kinds of jobs including farming. Some towns were small. Royal cities had large **temple** and **palace sites**. But the temples and palaces ran themselves. They had little to do with the life of the town.

## WORKING IN TOWNS

Most of the people who worked in towns worked outside. Houses were small, dark, and airless, so people spent as much time as possible outside. Men and women did different jobs. Women baked bread, brewed beer, and wove cloth. Men made jewelry, furniture, and shoes.

## MARKETS

Ancient Egyptians did not use money. They swapped the things they had made or grown for the things they wanted. Markets were set up in open areas near the river where trading ships docked and where the **warehouses** were. At the market, you could swap food, clothes, and cooking pots for the things you needed.

An Egyptian town

The pyramids, **temples**, **palaces**, and statues that are still standing give us an idea of the size of Ancient Egyptian buildings. Their carvings tell us how skillful Egyptian carvers were. But only the **tombs** remind us that Egyptian buildings were also colorful. Buildings were **whitewashed**. Then the most important ones were painted with bright colors and even covered with gold and silver.

## THE WORKERS

When a building was decorated inside or outside, different people did different jobs. Artists painted onto flat walls, not onto canvas or paper. First they drew the outlines of the pictures, planning them on a **grid** drawn on the wall. Artists had to obey rules about how to draw people and things and the colors to use. These rules were handed down over a long time. If there was carving to do, the stone carvers worked next. The carvers were followed by people who whitewashed the whole wall. Then more artists came to paint the carvings.

Tomb painting like this shows us how colorful homes could be. Houses would not have had hieroglyphs on the walls. Big houses might have painted scenes and people. Smaller homes might only have a pattern like the border at the bottom of this page.

This was written on a stone at the Temple of Amun at Karnak. It tells us how the temple was decorated:

This temple was built with white sandstone. It was decorated with gold. The floors were lined with silver. [*Silver was more precious than gold to the Egyptians*]. Its doorways were decorated with electrum [*a mixture of gold and silver*]. It is wide and large with many royal statues.

The Ancient Egyptians buried their dead with all the things they would need for the **afterlife**. This included furniture, clothes, jewelry, and food. It also included **shabtis**. These were model workers who would do the dead person's **corvée** in the afterlife. Important people also had models of things they would have owned in real life including workshops from their **estates**.

## WORKERS

All of these things for the dead had to be made by hand. Towns and estates had many workshops, some big and some small, where people made things for the **tombs**.

## SHABTIS

Shabtis were important. **Pharaohs** and important people had many beautifully carved shabtis. But even poor people, buried straight in the sand and not in tombs, were buried with a shabti. Some of the shabtis of poor people were so badly carved that they are just a rough outline of a person. They were probably made by one of the dead person's family.

A workshop on an estate

25

Craftsmen did not just make things for the dead. They made things for the living, too. Ancient Egyptians had far fewer possessions than we do, but they did need shoes, clothes, and furniture. Most of these things were made by men although women did most of the weaving.

## SETTING UP HOME

In Ancient Egypt, the most important part of getting married was setting up a home. Ordinary homes had a bed, one or two stools (only important people had chairs), one or two small tables, and baskets or wooden chests to store clothes and everything else. The wooden furniture was made by carpenters. There were craftsmen who made baskets, but people also made their own. People setting up home also needed a cooking stove, one or two pots to cook in, and one or two bowls to eat from. They ate with their fingers.

A **tomb model** of a weaving workshop from the tomb of Chancellor Mekter. This is a small workshop. A big **estate** would have had as many as 20 women working there.

AN ANCIENT EGYPTIAN SCRIBE WROTE ABOUT ALL KINDS OF TRADES TO SHOW THAT IT WAS BETTER TO BE A SCRIBE THAN ANYONE ELSE. HERE IS WHAT HE SAID ABOUT WEAVING:

The weaver is wretched inside the weaving house. The air is almost impossible to breathe. A missed day's work means a beating. Weavers cannot even see the daylight unless they give the doorkeeper food to let them out.

## EVIDENCE FROM THE TIME

Some **tomb paintings** show builders at work. There is no writing from the time that talks about exactly how builders worked.

A GREEK WRITER VISITED EGYPT IN 450 B.C. HE WAS TOLD HOW THE PYRAMIDS HAD BEEN BUILT:

It took 20 years to build the pyramid. It was made from polished stone blocks, none less than 33 feet (10 meters) long. It was built in steps. The base was built first. Blocks for the first layer were lifted with levers. They went up layer by layer. Finishing off began at the top and was worked down to the ground.

A tomb painting showing builders making mud bricks.

## NEW EVIDENCE

**Archaeologists** found builders' tools at Kahun. We can compare these tools with those in the tomb paintings. They also found stone cutting tools with **copper** and **bronze** blades. They tested the copper from these tools and found that the metals had been heated and mixed and that the tools were made in Kahun.

Tools for making mud bricks. They were found by archaeologists at Kahun.

# GLOSSARY

**afterlife** the place where the Ancient Egyptians believed the dead lived

**archaeologists** people who dig up and study things left behind from past times

**architects** people who plan buildings

**awnings** covers held up by poles to make shade outside

**bronze** a metal made by heating and mixing together the metals tin and copper to make a stronger metal

**copper** a metal that can be dug out of the ground

**chapel** where people went to pray to the dead or the gods

**corvée** all Ancient Egyptians who were not scribes had to do this work on the **pharaoh's** land for a set number of days each year

**courtyard** a large, walled, open space that is part of a building

**estate** a large piece of land with homes and farmland all run by the same person

**grain** types of grasses with fat seeds that are eaten. Barley, wheat, rye, oats, and rice are all grains.

**grid** lines drawn down and across to make a lot of the same-sized squares next to each other

**inundation** the time when the Nile River flooded each year and all the fields were under water

**officials** people chosen to work for the **pharaoh** who could tell others what to do

**palace** where a **pharaoh** lived

**pharaoh** the king who ruled Ancient Egypt

**priest** a person who worked in a temple serving a god or goddess

**ramp** a raised path going up or down

**scribes** the only people in Ancient Egypt who could read and write. Scribes ran the country for the pharaoh.

**shabtis** small models of people buried with dead people. They were supposed to do the dead person's work.

**shifts** each group of workmen worked for two months then rested for two months. The block of time they spent working was a shift.

**shrine** a place where a statue of a god or goddess is kept so that people can pray to it

**site** a particular place

**temple** a place where gods and goddesses are worshiped

**terraced** terraced houses are joined together by their side walls

**tomb** a place where someone is buried

**tomb models** tiny carvings or pottery shapes of people and things that were put in **tombs**

**tomb paintings** paintings on the walls of **tombs**

**warehouses** places where people store the things that they have bought or made to use or sell later

**whitewashed** painted all over with a layer of white paint

# INDEX

# MORE BOOKS TO READ

Allard, Denise. *The Egyptians*. Milwaukee, WI: Gareth Stevens Incorporated. 1997.

Clayton, Peter A. *The Valley of the Kings*. Chatham, NJ: Raintree-Steck Vaughn. 1995.

Steedman, Scott & David Salariya. *Egyptian Town*. Danbury, CT: Franklin Watts. 1998

Steele, Philip. *The Egyptians & the Valley of the Kings*. Morristown, NJ: Silver Burdett Press. 1994.